Dear Favorite Person

Things I Never Told You

BARSHA SALOME GURIA

quratebooks.com

Dear Favorite Person
© **BARSHA SALOME GURIA**
First Edition: 2023

© **Published by**

Qurate Books Pvt. Ltd.
14, Acron Watervista, Carona
V.P. Aldona, North Goa
Goa 403523, India
www.quratebooks.com

ISBN: 978-81-19263-54-7

Table of Content

Castle of Dreams

"Once there was a girl,
who was scared of love;
For the longest time
she kept her away.

But

Everything changed with time and fate
When the whole world went silent,
She made her own castle of love
locked up with her own dreams."

Beginning of an Endless Love Story

Years ago she met him;
A famous and a well known young man
He was handsome
And she was his Die Hard Fan .

She was simple ,
She was ordinary,
She didn't think it will work between them ,
But now story as such she has to carry.

Month of August

A bliss of solitude
It was her first time,
An evening with delicious mood
She texted him;

Oh !! what a miracle it was,
At that time she didn't think of him much,

Then finally on a bright morning,
He texted her back;
She was overjoyed,
But never knew it was a warning .

Emotions of everyday

For million years she was searching for you,
She realized it was something new,
Things got changed
Something strange happened;
Like thousand doors were opened.

It's Happening

She has dreamt a dream

Since she was a baby;

A wish she made

Deep from her heart;

On a happy morning

She awake, her dream started working out .

" I will come Tomorrow " He Said

Month of September

Hoping tomorrow will bring joy,

She couldn't sleep that night

Stared at the moonlight,

Dreaming of her boy.

Oh !!

She dreamt of them,

Wishing that 'our love never comes to an end '.

The Very First Meet

The first day they met,

She had her heart set;

She was waiting for the day to come.

Finally, Love came knocking at her door,

She was all surprised to see him close.

He whispered "now I want you more"

Ode to Love

He came to her Unexpectedly.

Everything took a turn for the better,
He made a place in her heart Slowly.

Made her addicted to talk,
Made her addicted to love,
He became a part of her life Effortlessly.

Her veins were frozen first,
It was his warmth , melted her Passionately.

She just carried away Naturally.
He drew a picture in her mind,
He warmed her up and made her Fly .

Union

She was beauty in all its glory, s

omeone very pure ,

An endless passion like all men dream of.

That first innocent surrender,

He embraced her with all his love,

He loved her like the moon.

She thought

together they were meant to be,

together their love spoke of until the time of eternity .

Lost in Him

She was living her dream,
lost in him . He gave comfort to her anxious chest,
He allowed her to take a rest.

"How long can you keep me here ?"
"As long as you wish ". he assured.
They wrapped each other up within a warm embrace,
Two hearts were beating one with the other ,
Both had begun a new one together.

His hands moved over the beauty of her,
And wanted to hold her close and near.
Stare into each others eyes,
He kept all his pain beside.

He painted her skin with his touch,
Her breathing became heavy and very rough.
They whispered sweetness in each other's ear,
He was very soft and dear.

That extreme pleasure filled the room,
Seeking union with the moon.

Those Eyes

She noticed those eyes

Oh…!! he has the most beautiful eyes,

more loyal than his words.

As she looked into those eyes, her emotions rise;

His eyes had the power,

They are majestic , full of secrets and beauty lies …!!

She Holds Her Breath

The man she was dreaming of
standing next to her,
In her quiet darkened room
they came near,

He looked at her once and more,
And she was fighting in her core,

Everything seemed to blend in one,
Slowly her fears had gone.

She was Afraid to Confess

She was dreaming,

Feel so fresh and exciting,

His smile to her was so inviting.

He was always on her mind;
She thought how lucky she was,
He was the type of boy, hard to find;
She was happy that they met,
Her heart was completely set;
Inside her it was his presence,
But she was afraid to confess;

Gift of Love

She Draw His Portrait

'I draw him

My pen moves on a blank page,

Picturing all the colors of your rage;

With each kisses,

I brush his skin;

I draw those eyes,

so gentle and bright;

I touch his hair

discover him so tender and fair,

With each cuddles

I bring him close and nearer;

If love is an art,

I draw him all the time

But I don't know where to draw the line.

That love had arrived
It was okay
for the first few weeks
Maybe it was months or years

The man who once danced in her dream

Was close to her,

So close that she could hear his breathe,

Yes it was hard to believe,

But she understood,

That love had arrived;

She thought how her dream came true,

Whatever it might be,

She knew in her heart,

That he was the man she was dreaming about .

An Endless Passion

As time flew and they grew close,

One day he handed her a rose;

An endless passion so easily shared,

With no regret or fear,

Every breath they take,

Sweet aroma of their love they smell;

Everyday of each passing moment,

She loved him with all her heart and soul;

Every little touch he gave,

Made her heart beat out of control .

Art of Love

She is beauty in all its glory,

an endless emotion in his story,

She is an art, she is a form

if love is rain , he was a storm;

Blanketing out the stars and moon

She was melting in his tune;

Raindrops were like sorrowful tears,

His soul was on her way like pioneers,

Together they were meant to be,

Together their love spoke of until the time of eternity !!

Dear Favorite Person

A true dream she prayed for

He always reminded her of her father,
she felt safe in his arms and then nothing could bother;
With him she was cured.

She lost her father, At the age of fifteen;
Her fate was written,
In the story of tragic,
And he was a miracle magic .

When he bent to kiss her face,
She said "you're my safe place".
She lay down to go to sleep,
He looked at her with love so deep;
He touched her head with his hand ,
She thought "I'm the luckiest in the land".

A Feeling of Belonging

It was a beautiful feeling

" Listen you are mine
and let our union be divine "
He said,

"I want to hold you , feel your touch
And this all is too much "
She replied ,

Two flames were lapping in each other,
Slowly he was making her believe in forever .

Why?

But did not know why?
She could not ask , she was too shy,

That feeling inside, she didn't understand.

There was something he wanted to hide .

Their First Movie

"You wanna catch a film with me?"
He asked,

It was supposed to be beautiful,
He just took her as a fool.

She trusted his precious promises,
But he didn't come
She was standing hopeless,

Then things turned sour,
Bad to worse, within hours.

Wind Changed its Direction

Something weird happened to him,

She was alone with her dream,

She wanted to fix everything,

But wasn't able to figure out anything .

Just a "No"

"Am I Disturbing You ?"
one day she asked,
Just a "No" came as a reply.

She was trying to get his attention,
But everything she tried
He cast her aside.

"How could you be so cold ?"
She couldn't take it anymore .

She was Wondering

She was wondering,
What would he think!
if she revealed
the dream, growing inside her.

She was wondering,
What would he say!
If she said
"everything that exists, carries me to you."

She was wondering,
What would he do!
"when I will say that I love you" .

This Love is Divine

Confused and searching for the right things to say,
She still didn't know why he was behaving this way.

Her heart wanted to believe him,
But mind knew he was lying;
She was in a war with herself,
But she kept on trying.

Then she didn't think twice,
She didn't go for any advice,
"He loves me and will be mine"
She believed that this love is divine.

A Very Special Day

It was his birthday,
she fixed her heart and decided to say
"I love you all the way".

She looked at the clock that tells the time,
It was 12 o'clock at night.
She wished him.

But ...
Within a minute there was a deep silence,
She got to know he belongs to someone else;
She couldn't believe her eyes,
"Are you in a relationship?" "Oh.. yes.!!"
He replied.

With that One Answer

"Why did you make love to me?

Why did you leave me for her?

Did you ever love me, was there a real moment between us?"

"With that one answer my whole world has changed,

You have found another

My love for you is a bother "

It was hard for her to believe,

That he was about to leave;

Her heart was shouting at his ear,

He was so deaf that he couldn't hear;

All things were so unclear,

She was in the darkness, where colors were blurred .

He Blocked Her Way

Next day she got shocked,
Found , she was blocked;

She tried to talk,
And called him with a single ring.
But could not , he blocked her way,
Love changed its glory day by day.

It was Dark

It was dark,

there was no light ... She was not feeling alright?

There was silence spread outside,

She was suffering from sleepless nights.

In her empty room,

She was weeping

And hoping it was just a bad dream,

It was taking too long to end the pain,

She was broken, still praying for him again.

It Wasn't Her Zone

All the blissful moments
that they spent together,
were suddenly kept aside.

Then he declared its not her,
And with his memories left her all alone;

She was shattered and broken into pieces,
She realized it wasn't her zone.

Ending of the Story

She fell in love and holded him in her heart,
And that was why it tore apart;

She was grateful,
With him everything was so beautiful,
But he wasn't faithful;

She made her own world of fantasy,
He destroyed her sanity;
That day
She came back to the reality,
The story came to an end finally .

I Close My Eyes , All I See is You

This hour
When the sun goes down,

Thinking of her favorite person
 she whispered to the moon,
" I've never thought it would come to this
How do I forget you ?
Why do I forget you?
I loved you for too long , in too many ways,
I may not be the girl for you,
But I remember us.
Our moments so genuine and true,
You will always live inside me
so close ,
When I close my eyes , all I see is you.

Time's Up

The hours when the shades are deepest in the heart,
Breeze from north carrying the mountains;

Now, I had closed the door upon my heart,
And wouldn't let anyone in;
I had trusted and loved only to be hurt,
But, that would never happen again;

I can see the frozen faces around,
When autumn's mournful moon was faint and pale;
And every bright star wore a cloudy veil,
Now Time is   Up
Made chaos and a space at last .

Already 6 Months Passed

Her lost love is back

"Can we turn the wheels of time back?"
A message came to her,
Her eyes were waiting for his text,
Her ears were craving to hear his voice.

"Is the love that we once shared, completely gone?"
Now he wants to get her back,
But she is far from his reach;

"Can I make my move,
Or just wait in this game
Should I tell him
Or keep my feelings inside ?"
She is struggling with it,
and time will say what is right …!!

"What Should I Do ?"

"Together we walked through the love's land a little way.

Together experienced some sweet lessons,

Then you left me, chose someone else,

And we parted away at the end of the day.

Again you want to walk through the same lane,

Take hand in hand , go together on our way.

Don't know

What should I do?

What should I say?"

To be continued....

9 788119 263547